T0417732

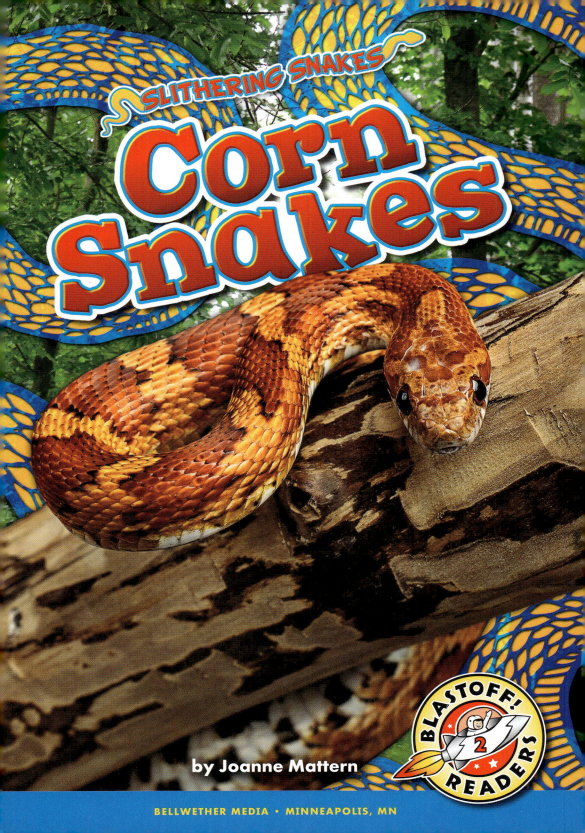

Blastoff! Readers are carefully developed by literacy experts to build reading stamina and move students toward fluency by combining standards-based content with developmentally appropriate text.

Level 1 provides the most support through repetition of high-frequency words, light text, predictable sentence patterns, and strong visual support.

Level 2 offers early readers a bit more challenge through varied sentences, increased text load, and text-supportive special features.

Level 3 advances early-fluent readers toward fluency through increased text load, less reliance on photos, advancing concepts, longer sentences, and more complex special features.

★ **Blastoff! Universe**

This edition first published in 2025 by Bellwether Media, Inc.

No part of this publication may be reproduced in whole or in part without written permission of the publisher. For information regarding permission, write to Bellwether Media, Inc., Attention: Permissions Department, 6012 Blue Circle Drive, Minnetonka, MN 55343.

Library of Congress Cataloging-in-Publication Data

Names: Mattern, Joanne, 1963- author.
Title: Corn snakes / by Joanne Mattern.
Description: Minneapolis, MN : Bellwether Media, Inc., 2025. | Series: Blastoff! readers: slithering snakes | Includes bibliographical references and index. | Audience: Ages 5-8 | Audience: Grades K-1 |
Summary: "Simple text and full-color photography introduce beginning readers to corn snakes. Developed by literacy experts for students in kindergarten through third grade"-- Provided by publisher.
Identifiers: LCCN 2024003105 (print) | LCCN 2024003106 (ebook) | ISBN 9798886870381 (library binding) | ISBN 9781644878828 (ebook)
Subjects: LCSH: Corn snake--Juvenile literature.
Classification: LCC QL666.O636 M375 2025 (print) | LCC QL666.O636 (ebook) | DDC 597.96/2--dc23/eng/20240208
LC record available at https://lccn.loc.gov/2024003105
LC ebook record available at https://lccn.loc.gov/2024003106

Text copyright © 2025 by Bellwether Media, Inc. BLASTOFF! READERS and associated logos are trademarks and/or registered trademarks of Bellwether Media, Inc. Bellwether Media is a division of Chrysalis Education Group.

Editor: Betsy Rathburn   Designer: Brittany McIntosh

Printed in the United States of America, North Mankato, MN.

Table of Contents

A Colorful Snake   4
Hunting Prey   10
Baby Corn Snakes   18
Glossary   22
To Learn More   23
Index   24

A Colorful Snake

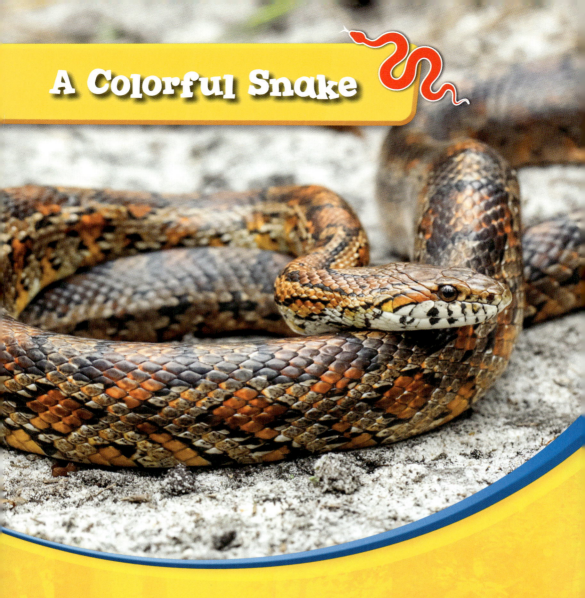

Corn snakes are **constrictors**. When they catch **prey**, they squeeze it!

These **reptiles** live in the eastern and southern United States.

Corn Snake Range

range =

Corn snakes grow up to 6 feet (1.8 meters) long.

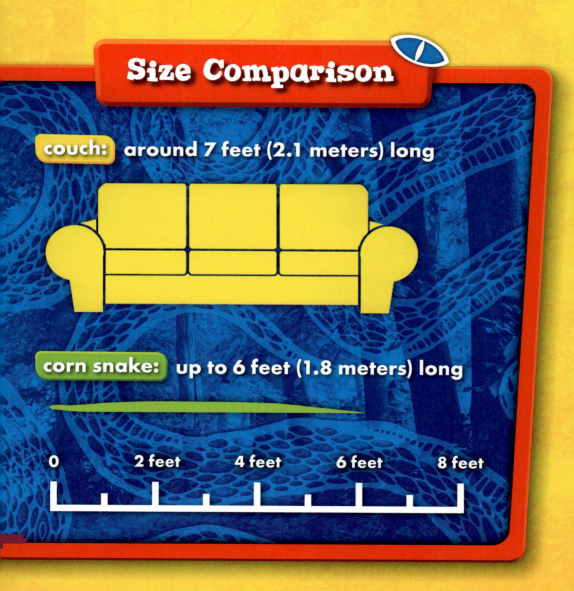

Their thin bodies weigh about 2 pounds (0.9 kilograms).

Corn snakes can have many different patterns.

Their red, orange, and black **scales** help them hide from **predators**. They have black-and-white bellies.

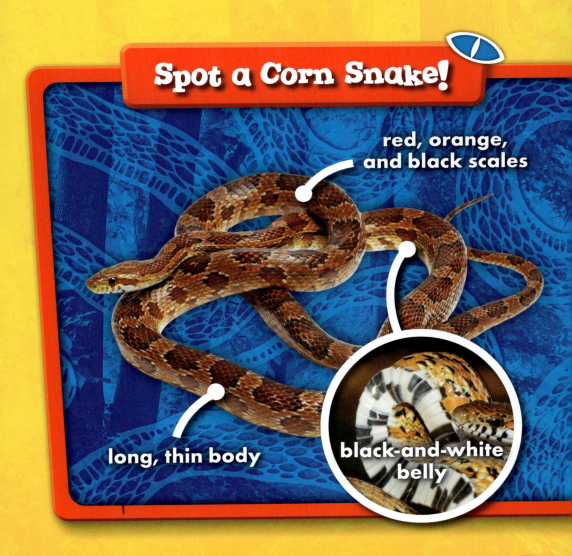

Spot a Corn Snake!

red, orange, and black scales

long, thin body

black-and-white belly

Hunting Prey

Corn snakes live in forests and fields. They stay under logs and rocks.

On warm days, they **bask** in the sun.

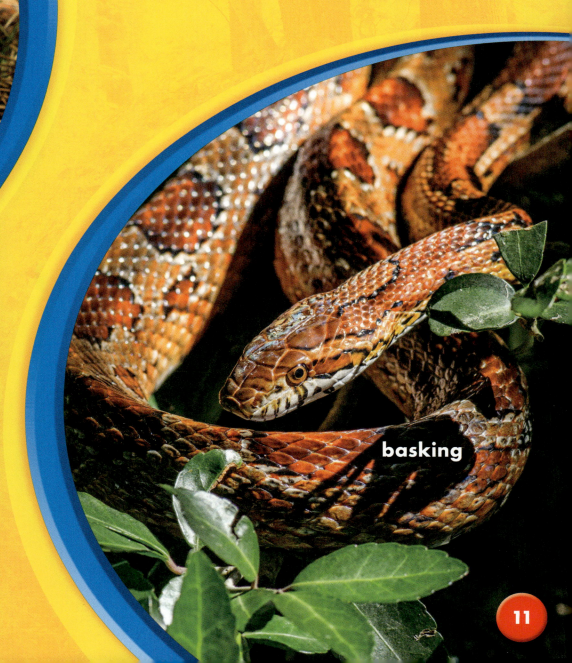

basking

Corn snakes **hibernate** in winter. They rest in logs or caves.

They are active again when the weather warms up!

Corn snakes eat every few days. They bite prey to catch it.

Then they wrap their bodies around the animal. They swallow the animal whole!

Corn snakes mainly eat **rodents** such as mice and rats.

They also eat birds, lizards, and frogs. They may climb trees to eat bird eggs!

Baby Corn Snakes

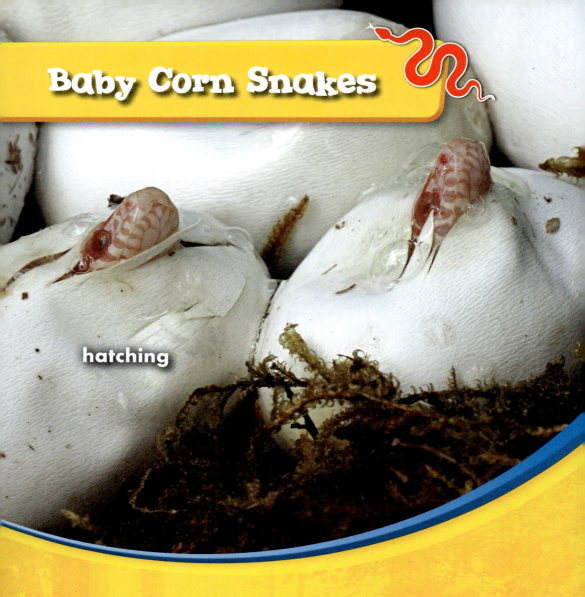

hatching

Female corn snakes lay up to 30 eggs at once. About two months later, the eggs **hatch**.

The babies take care of themselves right away.

Corn snakes grow fast! They **shed** their skin as they grow bigger.

These common snakes add color to our world!

skin

Corn Snake Stats

status in the wild: least concern

life span: up to 8 years

Glossary

bask—to lay in the sun; cold-blooded animals often bask to raise their body temperatures.

constrictors—animals that squeeze their prey

hatch—to break out of an egg

hibernate—to pass the winter by sleeping or resting

predators—animals that hunt other animals for food

prey—animals that are hunted by other animals for food

reptiles—cold-blooded animals that have backbones and lay eggs

rodents—small animals that gnaw their food

scales—plates that cover an animal's body

shed—to lose fur or skin

To Learn More

AT THE LIBRARY

Lock, Fiona. *Snakes Slither and Hiss.* New York, N.Y.: DK Publishing, 2023.

Mattern, Joanne. *What's So Scary About Snakes?* South Egremont, Mass.: Red Chair Press, 2023.

Thielges, Alissa. *Curious About Snakes.* Mankato, Minn.: Amicus, 2023.

ON THE WEB

FACTSURFER

Factsurfer.com gives you a safe, fun way to find more information.

1. Go to www.factsurfer.com.

2. Enter "corn snakes" into the search box and click 🔍.

3. Select your book cover to see a list of related content.

Index

babies, 19
bask, 11
bellies, 9
bite, 14
caves, 12
climb, 16
colors, 9, 20
constrictors, 4
eggs, 18
females, 18
fields, 10
food, 16, 17
forests, 10
hatch, 18
hibernate, 12
hide, 9
logs, 10, 12
patterns, 8
predators, 9
prey, 4, 14, 15
range, 5
reptiles, 5

rocks, 10
scales, 9
shed, 20
size, 6, 7
skin, 20
squeeze, 4
stats, 21
trees, 16
United States, 5
winter, 12

The images in this book are reproduced through the courtesy of: Luiza Kleina, front cover; Nynke van Holten, p. 3; Robert Hamilton/ Alamy, pp. 4, 9 (inset), 10, 19, 20-21; Andrew DuBois/ Alamy, p. 7; Supersport, p. 8; Eric Isselee, pp. 9, 22; Gerald A. DeBoer, p. 11; pokosuke, p. 12; PKimages/ Alamy, p. 13; Joesboy, p. 14; John Cancalosi/ Alamy, p. 15; George Grall/ Alamy, p. 16; SuperStock/ John Cancalosi Pan /Mary Evans Picture Library, pp. 16-17; Brian Moe, p. 17 (mice); Mr.Coffee, p. 17 (birds); samray, p. 17 (frogs); SuperStock/ John Cancalosi/ Nature Picture Library, p. 18; Grant Heilman Photography/ Alamy, p. 20.